T0065185

STOP IT! AND PRAY!

EXPERIENCING THE PANDEMIC COVID19

KRISTIE DAWSON

authorHOUSE®

AuthorHouse™
1663 Liberty Drive
Bloomington, IN 47403
www.authorhouse.com
Phone: 833-262-8899

Published by AuthorHouse 10/16/2020

ISBN: 978-1-7283-6817-7 (sc)
ISBN: 978-1-7283-6816-0 (e)

Print information available on the last page.

Any people depicted in stock imagery provided by Getty Images are models,
and such images are being used for illustrative purposes only.
Certain stock imagery © Getty Images.

This book is printed on acid-free paper.

Because of the dynamic nature of the Internet, any web addresses or links contained in
this book may have changed since publication and may no longer be valid. The views
expressed in this work are solely those of the author and do not necessarily reflect the views
of the publisher, and the publisher hereby disclaims any responsibility for them.

Scripture quotations marked MSG are taken from THE MESSAGE.
Copyright © 1993, 1994, 1995, 1996, 2000, 2001, 2002, 2003 by Eugene H.
Peterson. Used by permission of NavPress Publishing Group. Website.

Scripture taken from the King James Version of the Bible.

Scripture quotations marked NKJV are taken from the New King James Version.
Copyright © 1982 by Thomas Nelson, Inc. Used by permission. All rights reserved.

Easy-to-Read Version (ERV)
Copyright © 2006 by Bible League International

Scripture quotations marked NASB are taken from the New American
Standard Bible®, Copyright © 1960, 1962, 1963, 1968, 1971, 1972, 1973,
1975, 1977, 1995 by The Lockman Foundation. Used by permission.

Scripture quotations marked AMP are from The Amplified Bible, Old Testament copyright ©
1965, 1987 by the Zondervan Corporation. The Amplified Bible, New Testament copyright
© 1954, 1958, 1987 by The Lockman Foundation. Used by permission. All rights reserved.

Kristie Dawson is an Anointed Prayer Intercessor who loves to pray. She loves to minister the word of God so that people can be free. She does not compromise her relationship with God. She is married to Pastor Terrance Dawson, she has 2 beautiful daughters. She is the youngest out of four siblings. She loves to laugh and spend time with her family.

DEDICATION

First, I thank my God and Father, and My Lord and Savior Jesus Christ and the Precious Holy Spirit for His grace for giving me the anointing to be able to share one of the precious gifts to the body of Christ. "Prayer". *1 Thessalonians 5:17 KJV pray without ceasing*.

I thank my wonderful family. My husband Pastor Terrance Dawson, my daughters Lexie & Layla Dawson for your support and love. To my dad John Waye, and my mom Geraldine Waye and my four siblings, also to my father n law Bishop Arthur Dawson and First Lady Lucille Dawson and my other four siblings. My husband and my spiritual Mentors Bishop I.V. Hilliard and Pastor Bridget Hilliard. Also to all of our family members and friends thank you for your love and support. And to Pastor Monica McGowen, thank you for prayers as a Midwife.

INTRODUCTION

Prayer, is not an obligation! Prayer is a priviledge! Prayer is communication with God. Matter of fact it is the most important communication you can have with anyone. When we pray we give God legal access to get involve in our earthly affairs. Many people some "christians" have not really taken prayer as serious as it is. Prayer is powerful in its working **(James 5:16 MSG) The prayer of a person living right with God is something powerful to be reckoned with.** *Because it gives you supernatural help from heaven. Prayer allows you to release your worries and cast all your cares .***(Phili 4:6 KJV) Be careful for nothing; but in everything by prayer and supplication with thanksgiving let your requests be made known unto God. (1Peter 5:7 KJV, Casting all your care upon him; for he careth for you.)** *Many times when we are in trouble dealing with a problem, or bad situation, or needing an answer for something. We confusely make prayer our very last resort and this is after we have exhausted* *all of our natural resources that we felt or thought was helpful at the time. You have to stop it and pray! Whatever you are worrying about, or whatever you are feeling, or even thinking about . Let prayer be your beginning and your ending. Start off asking in prayer and finish by thanking God in prayer. It will make your life so much easier. Because now you have released whatever the problem was to God in prayer. If now for some reason you are still worrying about the problem, maybe because you really havent released it completely over to God, or you just choose not to trust Him to help you. But as the saying goes "If you worry why pray! If you pray why worry! So what are you gaining when you worry ? ABSOLUTELY NOTHING! When you worry and in fear it grieves God, and tells God that He does not have enough power to help you in your situation. Because if God is uttermost important to you, you know that He has the power to help you in any situation and He is your only help. So when you pray believe it and you will receive!.*

TROUBLESOME TIMES

2 Timothy 3:1-5 NKJV, But know this, that in the last days perilous times will come. 2. For men will be lovers of themselves, lovers of money boasters, proud, blasphemers, disobedient to parents unthankful, unholy. 3. Without natural affection, trucebreakers, false accusers, incontinent, fierce, despiser of those are good. 4. Traitor, heady, highminded, lovers of pleasures more than lovers of God. 5. Having a form of godliness but denying the power thereof: from such turn away.

The world is in a **PANDEMIC**!

Pandemic = Panic! Fear! Worry! Of a disease call coronavirus Covid 19

This pandemic caused schools, businesses, stores, restaurants, churches, sporting events to close. We were being shut in our homes when city curfew was mandatory. It was a history world making events, that never taken place before. Only time businesses and schools was close was because of threated weather conditions such as hurricanes, toronados, or in the north snow storms, or black ice. So, as we were in this season of a pandemic there was an epidemic of fear on the rise. Everyone was trying to figure out what to do, where to go, how to survive. Even those who were government leaders and even some christians as well did not have a clue what to do. Some did not obey the law that was set in motion. Many christian leader got citations for having church services with over 50 people in one place together that could easily cause the spread of the virus. So they were told by city leaders to close their church doors until futher notice. Many christian leaders were lead to use social media as a tool to be able to still minister the word of God, and see there members, to keep them encouraged during this pandemic.

In such a time as this, the world was in complete chaos. *(Psalms 82:5b (NKJV) All the foundations of the earth are unstable. (MSG) They havent a clue to what's going on. And now everything is falling apart the world is coming unglued.* From the White House to our house people was confused about almost everything. What am I suppose to do? Will I have food to eat? Can I leave my home? Will my children be ok? Will I still have my job once this is all over? Will I catch the coronavirus if I go outside? Do I need to purchase a month load of toilet paper? REALLY! We had to wear face mask when we left our home just to go grocery shopping or, even just to pump gas in our vehicles. Or even if you had a doctor, or dentist appointment they would check your temperature upon arrival to make sure you didnt have a fever, before they can service your medical need. I tell you this was a time that was unheard of, but it was really happening.

Our world as we know it was be shaken, turned upside down. Nothing wasn't the same and will never be. And with all this going on, did anyone **Stop It! and Pray!?**....................

The earth is waiting for us the children of God to make a move! Romans 8:19 Easy to Read Version; Everything that God made is waiting with excitement for the time when He will show the whole world who his children are. The whole world want very much for that to happen.

Heaven is prompting the children of God to take authority in the earth over this pandemic. We must dress ourselves with our spiritul armor and become front line soldiers in the spirtual realm. We must bow our knees in prayer and seek His face. We must be still and wait to hear His voice for instructions, and not to allow unfamiliar voices to speak empty words with no effects to us. **This is spiritual warfare!** This has physically attacked the earth realm with a epidemic disease that will take a lot of innocent people lives. So we are praying for medical science to come up with a vaccine to help fight off this disease in the natural. We are yet praying in the spritual realm that this virus will eradicated and be destroyed and die. So now we understand that... this means WAR! (**2 Corinthians 10:4 says the weapons of our warfare are not carnal, but mighty through God to the pulling down of strong holds 2Corinthians 10:4 KJV).**

How can we stop it? This disease is an enemy we are fighting against that we can not see but experiencing its deadly effects. I believe if we do what the scripture says in Matthew 18:19, if two or agree touch and agree in earth touching anything it shall be done. There has to be intercessors around the four corners of this globe and spirtual leaders who can hear the voice of God. That if we begin to pray and lift our voices at the same time around this nation God will hear from heaven and forgive our sins and heal our land. Whenever there was a famine in the land the prophets of old would always pray to God, or pray that God would speak to someone in the old testament to get instructions what to do. Its time for us to get on one accord and put aside our differences in color, race, religion, doctrine, and pray to the true and living God to get involved in the earth. Because there is a rollercoaster of problems thats has developed out of this pandemic and it is happening in every part of the world nothing or no one is exempt. From government to racism to unemployment and so many other things that is causing us to be divided. When we are divided we have No Power! to get the work done. We just sit around and let life happen and complain about everything and share our opinions about what we think with our lil two cents. Dont we know we need HELP? Where is the saints who trust in the Lord and not with lip service but with all their hearts? It seems like the time like never before. A sense of Jesus returning is more near to us then it has ever been. And we must get our house; our life in order. When he comes back will he find faith in the earth, or an undressed bride who is not ready for the wedding ceremony, where we become one with Him. If we pray I'm talking about really pray! We can stop this pandemic, not only with Covid19, but also the epidemic of problems that is pressing down weighing heavily in our world. For we have the victory in Jesus Christ!.

Prayer is now one our most important weapon we can use to be able to hear the father's voice as we battle in the spiritual realm to conquer this disease. We must as many times as the Holy Spirit lead us to turn down our plate meaning fast and pray. We must understand this is a different fight, and a different season we are in.

When we begin to cry out to God in prayer Help! Help!, Help Me! It is the most powerful prayer you can pray!. It's a solution to God that we need Him and He is our only hope. Dealing with troublesome times, our emotions sometimes always seems to get the best of us. We allow all kinds of illegal thoughts to ponder our mind. We become so vulerable and let our guard down that it allow the devil to see us as an easy target to aim his fiery darts to attack us. So then we become fearful, worried and depressed. But once you are feeling this way or going in that direction, you must immediately STOP IT and PRAY! Stop yourself from focusing on what's happening in the very moment or what's happening around you. **You must gird up the loins of your mind (1 Peter 1:13).**

SNAP out of it! and rebuke the devil for all the lies he is telling you and will continue to try to tell you if you volunteer to listen. Begin to speak the word of God and plead the blood of Jesus against the enemy. Now this is what you call a faith fight! You are fighting for your life, for your peace and sanity in the troublesome time you are experiencing in this pandemic right now, or even in your personal life.

In this troublesome time we must learn to trouble our trouble. We must pray and seek the Holy Spirit for help. Wait for Him to give us a strategic idea on what to do, because His ways are worth finding out. There are a few things He may lead you to do.

1. He may ask you to fast and pray
2. He may tell you to sow and seed and trust God.

3. He may tell you to begin to call those things that be not as though they were (Roman 4:19)

4. He may have you to wait and trust Him in the process.

But remember the saying goes " Trouble dont last always"! but its up to you how long you want the trouble to last in your life. See everything has a season with an expiration date on it to come to an end. (**Ecclesiastes 3:1 KJV To every thing there is a season and a time to every purpose under the heaven.**)

And we have to be encouraged and know that God will always come through for us. Psalms 34:19, read many are the affliction of the righteous but the Lord deliver us out them all.

Lets Stop and Pray!.............

Father I thank you, you are a present help in the time of trouble. Thank you Father you know what I am going through right now for nothing takes you by surprise. I ask you for healing and deliverance, and for your supernatural peace. And I thank you for the grace to get through this troublesome time. For I am more than a conqueor and victorious in Christ Jesus our Lord. Amen!

STOP IT! AND PRAY!

When was the last time you stopped and prayed about very important decisions you need to make in your life. Stopped and pray about who you are? What's your purpose in life? Stopped and prayed about your health? About your finances? Stopped and prayed about your job or career? Stopped and prayed about your family? and your future? Of course these are all important questions to ask yourself, but for you to get the answers you must Stop it and Pray!

So what is it? The *it...* the thing that is on your mind right now that you can't somehow get rid of . You eat with *it*, You shower with *it*,and you even go to bed with <u>it</u>. You somehow always talk about *it* with your friends. You pretty much take *it* with you where ever you go. If you need me to explain what the *it* is,. ok. Well, It's when you are worried, depressed, or stressed out about a problem, having anxiety, and letting negative thought patterns replay themselves in your mind. And it opened the door to allow the enemy to tell you lies and put you in a bad mood throughout the day and you cant seem to let it go and now you are in a state of bondage. And the enemy has the opportunity everyday to torment you with troubling thoughts that causes strongholds to develop in your life. But once you get tired of being sick and tired letting the enemy get the upper hand on you, you will stop it and pray! Pray and renounce any area of your life that you have accepted by allowing yourself to be in the state of (depression, stress, and anxiety). Now after you have renounce it and repent, let the Holy Spirit work in your heart and fill you with truth and freedom.

Stop It and Pray ! Is a command as **2 Chronicles 7:14 speak of; If my people who are called by my name will humble themselves and pray will I hear from heaven forgive their sins and heal their land.** In this verse God is commanding us to pray! He is telling us to humble ourselves and stop trying to fix everything on our own. For He has the masterplan, and he knows the process it will take us to get through our situation. Or He can do it supernaturally for us that no other power or natural help can do. We have to lean not to lean our own understanding, but always acknowledge Him and He will direct our steps Proverbs 3:5. God is the source of everything we need. So when you stop it and pray you got to believe that you will get results EVERYTIME! Praying in the spirit is where the answer is!.

What do I mean by praying in the spirit? I'm not talking about praying in tongues as I Corinthians 13 talks about, yes speaking in tongues is great and is a gift from God that you communicate with Him in the spirit. But praying in the spirit is when you pray God's perfect will, as the spirit leads you with words to say that get heaven's attention. When I mention to people about prayer I used to say "prayer is my second nature", but really it's my first nature, because to me prayer is **oxygen** that we need to live and function throughout the day. Just like a vehicle need fuel to function and go, just like a fish need water to live and swim, a bird need wings to fly. Well, with out prayer you are pretty much powerless, so we have to take prayer serious just as it is. Prayer is also the backbone of the church. Our backbone support our body in so many ways, but if a person breaks their backbone they are pretty much paralyzed. So prayer helps the church not to be paralyzed, unfit for service but to be a strong place of support for Christ. So let prayer be the jump start of your day!

COMFORT IN KNOWING

Romans 8:28 NKJV, And we know that all things work together for the good to those who love God, to those who are the called according to His promise.

It's just amazing to know how much God loves us. We know we love Him but, when we understand His love for us, there is nothing to compare to that love. Nothing can penetrate that love or stop His love from working on our behalf. God's love is powerful, patient, and permanent. Many many years ago a spirit of infidelity stuck his ugly head into my marriage. It was heartbreaking, it was embarrassing and somewhat confusing, because my husband and I were both christians, as I THOUGHT! But the devil found a way to deceive my husband because of the great calling he has on his life. Many times I wanted to throw in the towel and give up! Like, I did not sign up for this, I had so many natural voices and spiritual voices in my head telling me it was over. I could not understand because I'm a person who love hard and I love for real. (DONT PLAY! inside joke my husband and I only knows what that means). Well, we went through the process probably like any other married couple would have to do to save our marriage. It wasn't easy, but it was worth it!. My problem was I would always complain and always throw it up in my husband face. Until one day the Lord spoke to me. He said, "only way you are going to be heal from the pain, is when you forgive him!" It was so loud in my ears and filled with so much love. It immediately changed my life and I begin to see my husband as a new man. Because God didnt just love me, He loved him too. And at that moment I felt like God was using me to show forth His forgiveness even in a hard situation. WOW! And now I can happily say we have been married 23 years now as I'm writing this book. So I can truly say I experienced the comfort in knowing God's love when I stopped and prayed. To look back and see what the Lord has done in our lives, how God delivered us both. Praise God!.

Another situation that I experienced the comfort in knowing God's love, was in 2018, the death of my Dad. I really had to stop it and pray!

I remember it so clear as it happened yesterday. My dad and I had a pretty good relationship.I was the youngest out of 5 siblings. If I can really explain it "I was spoil" Not in a bad way I dont think, but in a way of being loved and taken cared of. Some people can spoil their kids in a way that they get them whatever they want, and try to become their friend and not their parent and ruin the child's life. But I was on the positive side of being spoiled. Well anyway my dad became really sick the end of December 2017 with a heart attack and stroke. I remember going to the hospital with mom and we prayed with my dad and his blood pressure slightly went down, but not completely to ease the pain he was experiencing. After a day or so he had to have a triple heart surgery. Overtime he got better and came home, but it was short lived and totally not the same. Unfortunately after 2 weeks he was admitted in the hospital and remained there, going back and forth from hospital to therapy. And finally he was able to come home 2 days before his death.

I NEVER EXPERIENCED DEATH, like that, so cold, so rude, and yet so permenant. "My dad! My dad!" was all I could say, It really wasnt fair to me, my mom and my siblings. We all had our selfish moments of course and still yet in disbelief. But I knew what I had to do. I had to gather myself together, stop it and pray! So as people was gathering I begin to pray quietly in the spirit, and as I did I felt the comfort of God's spirit strengthen me to help to assist my sibling. It was a peace that passed all my understanding and it helped to know God at a whole other level of His grace and love. So as I was being comfort through God presence I felt my strength day by day, and was able to accept to be absent from the body is that my dad is in the presence of the Lord.

Now your situation may not at all be like mines, but you can still take comfort in knowing that God is faithful and He loves you right in the situations you are facing right now. He can love you right out of it to deliver you. He is no respector of persons. If you will stop it and pray and let God speak to you like He did me, you will really get whatever you need from Him. He gives comfort to the comfortless, John 14:18 says, I will not leave you comfortless, I will come to you, and then He will wait on you. Thats just awesome to know that God loves us so much He was sent the Holy Spirit as our Standby and Jesus as our Chief Intercessor making perfect prayers for us to get it right so we can walk in our freedom that He has already paid the price for .

Lets Stop and Pray!......

Father I thank you now that you will comfort me with your out stretched arms and give me peace and healing, and my joy remain full. I will never be in bondage of this problem again according to Nahum 1:9 says the Lord will bring a utter end and the afflection shall not rise again the second time in Jesus Name Amen!

And this is the confidence we have that God will see us through this situation and anything in the future, because God is faithful, and our hope and trust is that He can and will help us and deliver us.

ENDURANCE

2 Timothy 2:3 KJV, Thou therefore endure hardness as a good soldier of Jesus Christ.

In our every day life we face ups and downs, trials and tribulations, and we wish it will all disappear and stop at once. But, unfortunately we dont live in a perfect world. Because probably in a perfect world some of us will probably still be complaining to God about just how perfect everything is. We will probably said something like this " Oh those trees are to tall and their leaves are too green. Or " oh no God the sky is just to blue, " and why does the grass feels like soft carpet, and so perfectly green, " Oh no God you must change this! So I say all that to make a point that there are somethings in life we are just going to have to endure. No it doesnt feel good at the moment, but its good for us. *David says in Psalms 119:71 NASB It is good for me that I was afflicted, that I may learn your*

statutes. James 1:2 NKJV, says my brethren count it all joy when you fall into various trials.

When we read the story about the disciples of Jesus and how they had to endure a lot of problems, and I'm sure at times they wanted to give up,because things was so hard for them. But Jesus gave them the same power he had to endure such problems that would come their way. In the book of Acts, it tells a lot about Brother Peter how he endure alot from evil religious leaders just because he wanted to preach Jesus where ever he went. He understood the calling and the mandate he had on his life. He knew that God was with him through it all. Sometimes God would send angels to assist Peter in his ministry, and put people in his path to help him along the way. The saints of God would interceding on his behalf to strenghten him that he will endure and not give up.

Now Jesus is the one and only person who ever lived that endured the worlds pain and sorrow of men. For He was the ultimate sacrifice to all mankind. He endured by being denied as the son of God. He endured as being our Lord and Savior, as the Healer, Teacher, Chief Intercessor. And when it came down to his crucifixion he stopped and pray! He instruct his disciples to pray with him of course as we know they could not stay away one hour to pray with him. But Jesus prayer was so intesify that He prayed with his very soul that this cup will pass Him, but it did not. But what God did through Jesus prayer was he strenthen Him to endure the suffering for all mankind so we all can be saved. So if Jesus went to the cross to endure just for us to be saved and He was all perfect without sin, of course we are going to have to endure somethings as well. But as He overcame so shall we. Amen!

Now what is it that you are having to endure?... Is it a bad report from the doctor? An unexpected financial situation during this pandemic? A disobedient child, or a abusive mate, a job loss, or a church hurt. None of these things feel good to have to go through. But honestly God is really working something out on the inside of you,a beautiful creation.

2 Corinthians 4:7-10 KJV But we have this treasure in earthen vessels, that the excellency of the power may be of God, and not of us. 8. We are trouble on every side yet not distressed; we are perplexed, but not in despair; 9. Persecuted, but not forsaken; cast down, but not destroyed; 10. Always bearing about in the body the dying of our Lord Jesus that the life also of Jesus might be made manifest in our body.

Endurance is strength that God gives when our natural strength is not enough. His strength causes us to not give up and lose hope for what He promised us, but gives us the ability to withstand hardships, and situations. We have to take on a mind set that it will not always be this way. Once you begin to realize that and stop and pray God will give you a plan of action to show you what steps to take for you to get the victory in your life.So as you endure the problem or situation you are in right now, know there is greater on the otherside and you are already looking better!

Let's Pray!

Father I thank you that you are a God who is full of mercy and grace. And I thank you, you will let your mercy and strength rest upon and help to me to endure any trial that I am facing facing right now. Lord, let me or forsake me, for you promise never to leave them or forsake them, and that this too shall pass in Jesus name, Amen!

Write down your struggles and ask the Holy Spirit to teach you how to pray in this season you are in. So you will know how to endure and overcome and be victorious in Christ.

THE POINT OF NO RETURN

Proverbs 26:11 (Easy Read Version) Like a dog that return to its vomit, a fool does the same foolish things again and again.

Why is it, when God has delivered us and brought us out of a hard place we seem to return there once again. So often people like the attention that they get from others when they are sick, sorrowful, or feeling sad. So they let their guard down once again to return to that old place where they was delivered from. Unfortunately a lesson that is not learn will revert back to it again. We must confess it, repent it and quit it!

Now after we have taken this first step, now we must stop it and pray and ask God to help us to renew our mind. We must apply the word of God daily to our lives. When Jesus deliver many people in the bible. One particular event comes to my mind. to my mind. The man at the pool of Bethesada who was paralyzed over many years. When Jesus showed up to the paralyzed man he asked him do he want to be made whole. The man immediately complained about his problem and what always happen to him. But the amazing thing that got my attention was that Jesus did not give any attention to this man's complaint. He immediately began to minister to the man healing and deliverance. Jesus said to him "see you have been made well, sin no more lest a worse thing come upon you.(What Jesus was telling this man do not return back to the thing that cause you to become paralize before) .After Jesus spoke these words this man was at a point of no return for his life. Just as Jesus spoke to this man he, is saying the same thing to us in our situations. That after He has healed us, or delivered us, or brought us out a bad situation and we are free, let us not offend Jesus by regurgitating back to what He has brought us out of. Because after one encounter with Jesus that should be enough!. See there is no gray areas with Jesus only black and white. Whatever He says or does it is final and it cant be revoked, or changed, and you can bank on it!.

Once you stop and pray about your problems and cast your cares over to Jesus, there is no reason for you to go back to what was, because you should trust that He is moving on your behalf. If you believe He is going to bring you out, you have to tell yourself you are at a point of no return. Your desire has to change for how you used to see yourself, or even how you see your problem. See once you begin to see yourself differently as Christ sees you, you dont have a desire to go back to that old way of thinking and doing. So even at the time your situation hasnt changed but the way you feel about it has. So that makes it better for you to be on your way to your deliverance. When we come to God and tell him about our problems, and we patiently wait for instructions, He gives us step by step what we need to do to get the victory in our life that we dont have to settle for less. But trust Him in the process. Amen!

Let's Pray!

Father in Jesus name, help us to humble ourselves before you and understand you have all power in your hand to deliver us out of any sitution we are in. Let us know that there is nothing to hard for you and there is no failure in you. For you are our Champion and King and you can and will deliver us because we are your children and we belong to you. Amen!

STAY ALERT

Matthew 26:41 NKJV Watch and pray lest you enter into temptation. The spirit indeed is willing but the flesh is weak.

Now you should be at a place where you are really taking the time to stop and pray, and not allowing things to overtake your focus. You must always be alert. Because in this christian walk the devil is not going to play fair. His only job is to steal, kill, and destroy you completely. So he will try almost anything to get you to not trust and believe God. **1 Peter 5:7-9 NKJV Casting all your care upon Him for He cares for you, be sober, be vigilant, because your adversary the devil walks about like a roaring lion seeking whom he may devour. (Amplified: seeking someone to serve upon and devour.) But if you stay alert you can resist him steadfast in the faith.**

See the devil knows your weakness and of course God does to. But you must ask God to strengthen you in your weakness to not allow the devil to overtake you and cause you to give into his lies. Weakness could be almost anything that take your strength and deprive you of your faith in God. Weakness could be : lust, the love of money, greediness, pride, self-righteous, low self-esteem,you are always second guessing yourself, comparing yourself to others. Fear, the fear of not having enough, and many other things. The enemy will tell you lies about something in one or more areas in your life over and over again to cause you to believe it. He will push the replay button just to distract you and cause you to doubt. But you must resist him steadfast in the faith. You must examine every thought that come to your mind by the word of God. And immediately speak out loud what God word says about you. "That you are fearfully and wonderfully made". "God will perfect all that concerns you". "God will provide everything that you will ever need". "He promise never to leave you nor forsake you". "For your life is in His hand". The more you confess the word of God out loud it will get inside your spirit and come alive. That's when you can have what you say, and **God is ready to perform His word on your behalf; Jeremiah 1:12.**

The more you spend time in the word of God and in prayer God will speak to you and you will be more aware of His presence and His voice. John 10:27, for my sheep know my voice and a stranger they will not follow. If a stranger speaks to you as the devil you will immediately recognize it, because it does not line up with the word of God. Rebuke it! and ignore it

Staying alert is when you are aware about what's going on around you and having discernment from the spirit of God what you should do. How you should respond or react in a situation. Mark 13:13, Take heed, watch and pray for ye know not when the time is.

Let's Pray!

Father God in the name of Jesus, I ask you that you will give the person who is reading this spiritual discernment. Let them not be ignorant of the enemy devices, but recognize him when he try to talk them out of trusting you. And to to stay focus and aware and not be easily distracted in Jesus name! Amen!

Now write down some things that cause you to be distracted. Put these things before God in prayer and ask Him to help you to overcome them in every way. That you may stop them and get the victory!

YOU ARE A WINNER !

1 John 5:4 KJV For whatsoever is born of God overcometh the world; and this is the victory that overcometh the world, even our faith. (Message Bible version), Every God-begotten person conquers the world's way. The world to its knees is our faith. The person who wins out over the world system is simply the one who believes Jesus is the Son of God.

God create you to be a winner to live with purpose. A winner, not in the aspect of just winning a prize, or receiving a trophy, or a ribbon in a competition, but to win in life. When you realize that life is much more than what you can see with the naked eye, you will so dililgently take time to stop and pray. Get instructions get instructions from God on how you should live in this earth. And win in every area of your life. See God is your life coach and He will show you the ins and outs out of this life, and He is cheering you on. He show you what play to make to win. Just like a natural coach. He coach his players on defensive and offensive play to know how to win a game.

When things get hard a winner is a person who does not give up! But they keep at it until they have accomplished their goal. Any athletic will tell you anytime they are preparing for a sport event.Their mind is always set on winning. It really doesnt matter who the opponent is, or sometime the rules of winning is always on their mind. They have to train themselves even in unpredicted weather conditions. They must eat a strict diet so their bodies will remain strong. But one of the most important thing to help them to stay focus and win is their confidence. After all the physical preparation they have done it's really no use if they dont have their minds set with confidence in the game to win.

Well, in life we deal with all kinds of problems from our health, finances, relationships, job, and family. And when these problems confront us we feel like we are about to lose in life. But we must chose to keep our head in the game, and not focus on the problem, but pray and stop these from overtaking us. I can recall a few years ago about a dream I had. Well this man of God I knew who was pretty cool and was a great example to my husband and I. He had went home to be with the Lord a few years back. And in my dream he was trying to get to me for some reason. In the dream I did not want to see him, because I knew he was dead in real life. But in this dream he was determined to get to me. Well I would run here and there trying to get away from him. When I felt like I was safe....... he came out of no where from behind me and hugged me like a big bear hug!. Oh no is all I could say! like ok, You got me! You got me!

So he said to me "dont you know why I'm chasing you right"?! I said "No"! He said there is a BIG 'W' on the back of your head that means you are a winner!. You will win in everything in life. You have dealt with so many things at such a young age. But you shall win, win in life. I woke up out of that dream with a loud praise with a hallelujah on my lips. I literally had to leave out my bedroom and go outside in the garage and give God all the praises at 3' oclock. God want to tell you the same thing. When problems arise in your life the only thing you are you supposed to do is Stop it & Pray!. And you shall win over everything in life. Because you are a winner so begin now to stop it and pray and get the victory and WIN! WIN! WIN!

Printed in the United States
By Bookmasters